VIEWS FROM THE HILLS

*An illustrated country diary
from North Pembrokeshire*

by
Tony Holkham

Volume 1 : 2011

Views from the hills
An illustrated country diary from North Pembrokeshire
Volume 1 : 2011

First published 2012
Words and pictures © Tony Holkham 2012

OTHER BOOKS BY TONY HOLKHAM

For more details see www.tonyholkham.co.uk
All books are available as e-books and/or in print
Visit Amazon to see them all together

Views from the Hills 2 (2012)
Views from the Hills 3 (2013)
Ernest Briggs and the Great War
   Perspectives from 1928 and 1996
Beating the Big One
   Alan Priddy's North Atlantic journey by open boat
Challenge
   Round-Britain sailing adventure
Money management made easier
   A practical handbook for ordinary people
Label Writing and Planning
   A guide to good customer communication
Sonnets
Abandoned tales
   Short stories

AND IN THE PIPELINE...

Being Sparky
   Some people think I'm only a dog
Bobs and Bits
   A look at life through fiction, fact and verse

To Suzy:
for the love of my life

and to Sparky:
for the love of laughter

CONTENTS

VIEWS FROM THE HILLS

An Illustrated Countryside Diary

Volume 1 : 2011

Preface

Ideas are like buses: you wait for ages, then several come along at once – sometimes so fast you cannot remember them all before you can commit them to paper or screen. So it is one of my greatest pleasures in life to be able to write a countryside diary, not to any deadline or prescribed routine, but when an idea comes that is worthy of recording.

The contents of this little book were circulated piecemeal to friends and relations over the course of the year, and their positive and encouraging responses were what decided me to publish. So it's their fault.

All the original 'Views' are here, together with a few more thoughts that have occurred to me as I compiled them into what I hope is a coherent volume, and a few more pictures that may have merit (but that's not for me to judge).

As a writing adviser in business and the private sector, I am conscious of the fact that producing this work as an e-book is a necessity in this technological day and age. With printing costs going through the roof, and the likelihood of having a book published by a mainstream publisher approaching ever-closer to zero, I am also aware that the e-book route will be taken by many hopeful writers with the result that the market is swamped with many books that should never have been published at all.

I just hope this little tome of mine is not one of those… You decide and, if you will, let me (or Amazon) know.

If you would like to contact me for practical help with your writing or just moral support, you are welcome to do so. Email me at tonyholkham@gmail.com or go to my website www.tonyholkham.co.uk for advice.

Tony Holkham, Pembrokeshire, March 2012

About the author

I was born in Mitcham, Surrey – now London – in 1948 and my mother started teaching me to read and write before I went to school. Throughout my school years I learned to love learning through reading, and learned to love writing through practising the art at every opportunity.

While I wrote a great deal, in many different genres, it was always as a hobby, but I always dreamed of becoming a recognised writer. By the time my first short story was published in 1977 in the Evening News I felt I was a little nearer to my dream.

But there was an income to be earned, and writing was always a living for a very few. After many years in industry working with scientific and technical literature, and product labelling and information, I finally plucked up the courage to leave full-time employment and become a writing consultant, teaching businesses and private individuals how good writing is the key to good communication and relationships. I published a business book on the subject in 1996 and have since published several other books, as well as contributing articles to a wide range of periodicals.

These days I am working on a number of new projects (see next pages) as well as offering tailor-made online writing courses for people who want to learn the craft.

My love of the countryside has been a large part of my life for as long as I can remember, but it is only recently that I have begun to write about it seriously. I hope this little book is a reflection of the deep reverence I hold for the natural world and will, in some small way, stimulate the same reverence in others.

VIEWS FROM THE HILLS

An Illustrated Country Diary

Volume 1 : 2011

by
Tony Holkham

OUT-FOXED

February

Sitting on the stile halfway up Frenni Fawr to drink in the views across the Preselis to Dinas Head last August, out of the corner of my eye I saw a movement in the field. Knowing that any sharp movement would betray my presence, I turned slowly to see what it was. It was a fox, walking casually through a flock of totally unconcerned sheep.

This was not the sort of fox I used to see when I lived in a town for a few years; this was a country fox – sleek, glossy, well-fed and completely confident in his natural home.

I saw him again a few days later, this time on the footpath leading down from the hill, my attention distracted by the summer fruits in the hedgerows interspersed with the yellow of the gorse mixed with the purple of the heather. He ambled down the track for a few yards then with effortless ease and in one bound topped the bank and disappeared.

Sparky, my inquisitive but short-sighted Jack Russell, came upon the scene moments later and knew by his powerful sense of smell exactly what had happened. He took two bounds to reach the top of the bank and paused for a moment. I called him down because I thought if there was a confrontation he might not get the better of it.

On neither of these occasions did I have my camera with me, a frequent indicator of my failing memory for small things, so I could not record them. So I determined – with camera – to try to meet the fox again. The next two walks were fox-less. Either he didn't want to be seen or was elsewhere and, not having provided me with an itinerary, his routine remained a mystery.

It was therefore several days later that I encountered him again. Sparky had gone on ahead, and at some point in our climb the fox had picked up his scent. He knew I was there, of course, because he would have heard me tramping heavily up the path from some distance away, and he could see me intermittently from the field he was in. But he could not see my short companion and so took to slightly higher ground, straining his neck to get a glimpse of his canine cousin and, as far as he knew, intruder.

He tracked us by sight for half a mile, passing easily through the fences that separate the hill fields, sitting on his haunches in plain sight while he waited for us to catch up. Still he could not see Sparky, and at last he came to the bank by the path and peered through.

My camera, so often regrettably forgotten in the rush of looking for the seemingly myriad walking paraphernalia, was raised and ready. He and I locked eyes for a few moments, and he did not flinch at the click of the shutter. With immense satisfaction I continued up the path. When we reached the open ground above the stile, the fox finally saw Sparky, presumably decided he was no threat, and turned and loped back down the hill to resume his rounds.

In the meantime, Sparky had found some of the fox's scat and rolled in it. When we got home, I hosed him down, washing away the (to me) foul smell, and the smile from his face.

I saw the fox once more before autumn made the ground too soggy to walk without Wellingtons, which are not my idea of comfortable footwear; this time he was high up on the hill amongst the rabbit warrens, almost indistinguishable among the dying bracken, and again he saw Sparky who remained oblivious. Sparky must wonder: who is this strange dog that I smell but never see, and whose scat is heaven-scent? Somehow I doubt that the fox feels the same about his, but you never know.

And now spring has come round again, and the rain clouds from the Preselis less frequent, Sparky and I will soon renew our acquaintance with Frenni Fawr and – who knows? – say a silent 'hello again' to that most elegant and confident of predators whose presence reassures me that the countryside I love is still stimulating, wild and free.

Footnote:

There have always been dogs in my family, if not in my household, and I never cease to marvel at the bond that can exist between human and canine, exemplified by kindness, mutual respect (and a clear understanding of who is the boss!). Foxes may be closely related to dogs, and have been kept as pets, but there is a wildness in their eyes that sets them apart from our thoroughly domesticated friends. In a country devoid – unless you believe the hype – of large predators, the country fox is a magnificent animal, and I never see one without a thrill in my heart.

You will read more about Sparky, our constant companion and court jester, whose addition to our home has brought joy to our lives and more laughter than we could ever have imagined.

DON'T LOOK DOWN?

2 April

Birds are everywhere you look. From the majestic red kites and buzzards to most members of the crow family, from seabirds to seed-eaters, our North Pembrokeshire skies are so full of feathered interest that we sometimes forget to look on the ground. The dunnock, when I go into the garden, barely looks up from foraging about the bases of the shrubs, and the sparrows know the difference between a dog and a cat; the former they ignore, the latter they scold. The robin, who has been singing almost continuously for two months, day and night, is looking for a nest site among the ferns and old pots.

Watching the ground-feeding birds yesterday, I was surprised to see a baby rabbit in the garden. No bigger than a teacup, it searched under the *Pieris* for tasty morsels, and I only urged it away when Sparky our Jack Russell emerged from under his blanket to do the same. A case of not letting the dog see the rabbit.

It was the first rabbit I have seen since moving into our Blaenffos bungalow last autumn; I felt sure there must be some in the banks of the fields behind our house, so was delighted to see this one. I now know I have to take extra precautions to protect the vegetable crop which is already emerging in the greenhouse.

In this cold spring, there has yet been little evidence of insect life, save for a few cluster flies in the conservatory and the odd hesitant bumble bee. It has always fascinated me how insects are completely confounded by glass – it must seem to them like the force-field of science-fiction imagination. However, I know that a few more days of warm sunshine will tempt out the butterflies that have been quietly and patiently pupating in the dark corners of the garage.

We were honoured by a visit from seven goldfinches this morning; such a contrast to the dull-coloured but feisty sparrows, almost as if they were on their way to a carnival. I know it may be weeks before we see them again, but they will be back. Other finches and tits are a daily delight, and I look forward to the sound of the thrush beating snails against the stones – then spring will truly be here.

When we lived under the shadow of some dense woodland a few years ago, I counted 55 species of birds in or around the garden. Here, at an altitude of 700 feet, there are fewer species but on the whole they seem healthier and are less inclined to flock to the feeder, preferring instead to find their own food in the surrounding rich farmland.

If I am distracted from my keyboard by movement on the ground outside it reminds me that while we may naturally think of birds as creatures of the air and the trees, it is only half the story; even the pair of tumbling, croaking ravens high above cannot for long distract me from the wildlife that thrives beneath our feet.

Footnote:

Despite looking out across fields as often as I can, I have never seen – apart from this one – a rabbit in the village. And yet there must be some. Frenni Fawr, on the other hand, has plenty, and there are constant flashes of white scut as they dive for cover on seeing the dog. So the baby rabbit was a mystery and the incident has not reoccurred.

This is in sharp contrast to when we lived only a few miles from here and had a much wilder garden; there, I was privileged to be adopted by this young rabbit who shared the weeding with me from time to time.

CYRIL WAS HERE (I THINK)

11 May

Cyril Wiggle is very disappointed with his internet coverage. Anyone would be with only 40 hits, and one of those an unrelated bicycle shop. He considers himself worthy of the hundreds of thousands of hits achieved by putting almost anyone else's name into Google's search box.

If he were here, I would have to point out a few home-truths. Firstly, he is too mean to pay for his own website and has left it to me to be his publicity agent. Secondly, he doesn't need an internet presence at all, because he can never be contacted - preferring to just turn up wherever and whenever he feels like it.

Thirdly, he has created so much havoc with his practical jokes and acidic comments to the media, no stone should be unturned to keep him away from the internet at all costs.

But then, I would not have time to berate him on his internet complaint because I knew that by the time I had thoroughly dressed him down (supposing I should ever have the opportunity) regarding the shameless way in which he masqueraded as a hairdresser for several years (the salon in question actually had nothing to do with him) he would be gone again to mastermind mischief elsewhere.

The only reason I mention him at all, and thereby increase his internet hits to 41, is because of a curious coincidence. Something caught my eye as I was putting out the recycling last week, a shiny object half buried by the gravel outside our front fence. It was a descant recorder, the type that children love and parents hate. I assumed it had been lost by one of the children who play in the road after school so I left it in a prominent position and expected the owner to have recovered it by the next day.

The next day the children played as usual, but in the evening the recorder was still there, and a thought hit me between the eyes like the early morning sun reflecting off the white washing on the line. I remembered that Cyril was very fond of the recorder – not as a musical instrument, but as a weapon of revenge. It went like this – someone annoyed him and, if they had children, a recorder would be sent to each child as a present; if they did not have children, the neighbours' children would be so treated.

So was Cyril here? When we are led to believe he is on his way, he never arrives. When we least expect him he is most likely to turn up. And if he does turn up and we are not at home, he is more than likely to leave a cryptic visual message (last time it was our house number unscrewed and replaced upside down) rather than what most normal people would do, which is leave a note on the door.

I don't really know why I'm relating this at all. Whenever I mention Cyril, my friends give me that quizzical "And your point is?" look. So I suppose that is the point.

Footnote:

You may well wonder what this piece has to do with the countryside. Well, everything. And nothing. Cyril dislikes the countryside intensely; to him, the thought of Wellington boots (since he saw a girl in Spain wearing them with a bikini) are a distinct turn-off. The only rabbit he will entertain is one with plenty of chilli. A tree is something you sit on after mysterious things, involving a lot of noise and – heaven forbid – sweat, have been done to it. He has, however, been seen feeding the birds, and when I pointed out that birds are part of the countryside, his immediate response was that he was trying to encourage next-door's cat so that he can trap it and take it across the river where he feels there will be much grander and more profuse patio roses to crap on.

To Cyril, the countryside is an expanse of wilderness between two towns; take him to a spot where there are breathtaking views and he will point to the only building to be seen and inquire, with a note of horror in his voice, whether that is the nearest pub. Speak to him of corollas and he will tell you he has driven several of those; try to impress on him the glory of that beech and you are back to Wellingtons.

I cannot think of Cyril without thinking of Mr Toad, but there would be little point in mentioning that. For Cyril to read a book, let alone one that so epitomises the countryside, the sky would have to fall.

MONTE CARLO OR DUSK

29 May

It seems odd to consider the Monaco Grand Prix and a sunset in one train of thought: the brash and raucous excitement of one and the quiet serenity of the other. Yet that is how the writer's mind works – always looking for juxtapositions that seem to make sense of the world.

I could not possibly afford to go to see them race round the streets of Monte Carlo, but I don't mind. I went to three Grands Prix in this country – many years ago now – and I have never forgotten the true sound, however much it is dulled by our ancient television. Nor the smell of burgers and fried onions. I was there for *that* race at Donnington in 1993 and often when the Preselis dump their wind and rain on us as they do today I am reminded of it. Memories are made of this.

But it costs nothing to watch the setting of the sun. We are fortunate that, at this time of the year (when the weather permits) we can view the spectacle from the comfort of an armchair. As the disc drops below the hill – always much more quickly than I expect – the colours of orb and sky change rapidly through most of the warm and cold hues of the spectrum and light up the edges of the clouds. I am as spellbound as I am during a motor race.

Our snoozing dog cares nothing for the sunset. To him it is not a thing of beauty, just a sign that another day is coming to a close. He does not think of tomorrow. He may hear the blackbird casting his song into the west wind and the house martins chattering incessantly in their high-octane search for insects. He may see the lone crow plodding wearily among the docks in the meadow. He may sometimes think of burgers (he was once a stray), but he does not need these constant reminders of the continuity of life to fuel his eternal optimism. I do.

But above all it is the very incongruity of the motor race and the sunset that tells me all is well, that life is predictable, that we can look into the future with hope. The race will be spectacular as always, and the sun will rise again tomorrow. The beauty of the cutting edge of technology in the one and the mystical qualities in the other tell us that life is special. And the special place for humanity, to be given the ability to appreciate these things – is that not a magical thing, too?

So is the tear in my eye from the beauty of it all, or is it just the brightness of the light?

I wish that dog would learn to relax...

THOSE ENCOUNTERS OF THE BIRD KIND

23 June

I noticed a curious thing yesterday; the house martins were very agitated, and the reason was that several sparrows had taken up positions on the roof apex directly above the nest. I have never seen this behaviour from sparrows before, and the martins were certainly not impressed. It took a number of dive-bombing attempts before the sparrows were eventually driven away.

It was not the only curious event. At some time in the morning, a grey heron flapped lazily overhead, the first I have seen on our hill. Soon afterwards, a pair of black and white woodpeckers landed on the trunk of our palm and pecked among the dead leaf ends for food. Both birds had brilliant red crowns and so were presumably a pair of juvenile greater spotted woodpeckers and in fact I recognised the familiar "chack!" call as they approached.

What was surprising was that it was sparrows, and not woodpeckers, that were distressing the house martins, as woodpeckers are known (only recently to me) to prey on other birds' eggs and young.

In the wake of a serious chest infection I managed to drag myself up the hill this morning. I have never felt so relieved to reach the stile, and the dog, with his customary impatience, sighed and prepared for the wait. I was surprised (and so was he) how quickly my breath came back and we trudged on a little further, he looking for I have no idea what, and me listening to the skylarks, and occasionally seeing them.

It was when I passed a gate and in a meadow of purple-hazed grasses a flock of about twenty birds suddenly took flight, wheeled twice, and settled again, I remembered I had forgotten both my binoculars and my bird book, needed for just such an eventuality. It would have been no use taking a picture – they would have appeared as identifiable as a swarm of flies in my shaky hands – so I did not know what they were.

And then a revelation hit me, quickly followed by a resolution. The former was that I did not need to know what they were – and the ardent twitcher will perhaps faint dead away at this – and the latter was that I did not need to bother to find out. As a lifelong identifier of things, questioner of things and need-to-knower of things, this came as quite a shock to me. It was like suggesting to the village busybody that they didn't need to look out of the window.

From now on, I shall just watch, listen and remember. Should I discover a name, I may note it in my bird book, but I shall not trouble myself to look for it. For too long I have been saddling – and possibly diluting – these astonishing visual and aural delights with labels and, as Garfield pointed out the other day, admittedly in another context: "Who has time for labels?"

Labels? That's another story.

Come to think of it, there is no reason to be surprised at having a revelation – no sooner had the revelation that the dog has no interest in the sunset (see the previous entry) occurred, than he made me out a liar by doing just that which I thought he wouldn't.

Footnote:

I wrote a book about labels. It was my first real book, published by a real publisher, printed on real paper. Now, you may think of labels as a dry subject, and not for the likes of most people, but I have it on good authority that even a business book can be good to read if it is entertaining, and I certainly tried to make it that. I was probably one of the leading product information specialists in the world at the time and my book is still, after all these years, on sale (at Amazon and many other sellers), and there is even a Kindle edition now. Such progress.

Labelling, as a means (often the only means) of communication between manufacturer and consumer, is fundamentally a writing job, yet so many – in fact most – companies leave the job to whoever has the time and do not take a professional view of it at all. I have long since ceased to try so hard to make my voice heard in this respect; and yet the press still carry almost daily examples of schoolboy howlers on labels and in leaflets, manuals and other how-to documents. It is a sad fact that since my book was published in 1996 it has not brought me riches.

So I now write about the countryside, which has – and I'm not speaking of money.

OUT TO GRASS

29 June

Notwithstanding my comments on 23 June, I did identify a solitary swift flying over the house today, ignoring the evening sky full of house martins. His solitary, direct passage was unusual in itself; there are plenty around the area, but this is the first I have seen in this part of Blaenffos. The sparrows still sit menacingly on the roof above the martins' nests.

But the drone of hay-making machinery through the daylight hours is what has had my attention this week, and my attention is drawn away from birds and to grasses. These wonderful and ubiquitous plants, hardly noticed, are the ever-present backdrop to all other life in the country. And now they are flowering as only grasses can.

Seen individually, and out of their true dimensions, they are the trees of the smaller world, bending to wind and rain, and even more varied in colour and form than their giant botanical cousins.

When I was a young teenager, a schoolmaster colleague of my mother's gave me a collection of grasses, the specimens neatly stuck to sheets of paper annotated with their common and Latin names, and it was yet another example of the simple gifts which have instilled a lifelong love of all natural things. He also gave me a collection of butterflies, including the I believe now-extinct (in the UK) mazarine blue. I continued with both collections for a time until other teenage distractions came along and took rather urgent precedence.

Now, of course, it is not the done thing to collect butterflies, as they are becoming quite rare. On the contrary, I hope to encourage more with some buddleia plants a kind friend has propagated for me. They will not just attract butterflies, but hundreds of other insect species – food for the insect-eating birds such as the house martins. I am also allowing nettles and other wild food plants to grow, and soon I will be collecting seed from the roadside flowers (before the vandals come and scythe them away) to spread in the quiet corners of the garden to feast the eyes next spring.

But although the flowering plants are lovely, it is the grasses in their sheer profusion that I find most fascinating. It is almost without thinking that we pull up the grasses that have taken root in the patio, on the back door step and even in the tarmac drive; sometimes, though, it is fun to leave them for a while to see what beautiful specimens they will become.

Footnote

Sparky, while seemingly sanguine about having to go outside to do his business, does like to do so on grass. To go into this in any more detail would constitute too much information; suffice it to say that when we moved here I seeded a small area of the gravel to accommodate him, and I have to say it was very well-received.

Next to this tiny lawn I had inserted a metal bird-feeding pole from which hung various patent receptacles for hanging bird seed. After a few weeks, some vigorous flag leaves appeared, followed by a large number of barley plants which rapidly grew to more than a foot high and developed seeds of their own.

This, I thought, with a satisfied smile, is free bird seed for the winter. No, it wasn't. Dogs have a propensity for eating grass from time to time for medicinal purposes, and also to lift a leg to anything higher than three inches from the ground. The barley didn't stand a chance.

LOOKING ON THE BRIGHT SIDE

12 July

I must admit to finding it difficult to understand why the main road through the village, and even our little cul-de-sac, is flooded with yellow light from dusk to dawn. There are no pubs or clubs to disgorge tottering, exuberant youth into the damp night air; the village shop closes at 7pm; the majority of the vehicles on the road at night are heavy lorries whose cabs are festooned with up to ten powerful spotlights. Songbirds lose sleep, unaware that night has fallen; insects beat themselves against what they believe to be the moon, their assignations cut cruelly short by the intelligent bats; and this is not to mention the criminal waste of energy and the light pollution that hides the majesty of the night sky.

The lights are so bright even the departed souls in the graveyard must have difficulty resting in peace.

I have no objection to public lighting *per se*; a few twinkling lights on the hill contrasting the distant dusk rainstorm can be quite magical; it is the floodlighting that mystifies me. While we lived in Hampshire for four years, night in the town grew ever brighter; we could have sat in the front garden and read a book; no curtain was thick enough to shut out the glare; no argument by the local council was ever in the slightest convincing. Here in West Wales, about as rural as you can get, there is no justification whatsoever for this sad trend that elsewhere in our beleaguered nation is finally beginning to be reversed.

There we are, I've had my say. The sodium glare seems to be what the majority of people want, so I must accept it. I can at least enjoy the blackbird and robin singing their hearts out at one o'clock in the morning; I can be mesmerised by the staggeringly beautiful moths that settle on our windows to recover their energy; there are always compensations; there is always a bright side: and how ironic that is in this case.

It is too cold to read in the front garden here. I am still trying to understand how the altitude affects the growth of plants that provide food for the table; why the wind shrivels the beans and the beetroot, but seems not to affect the peas and carrots, and why we cannot eat enough raspberries to keep pace with their manic production. Although the heat haze over the hills to the north west tells a different story, the air here is cool in contrast to the sun's warmth because the life-giving rays are filtered through a light grey cloud cover.

There is a different insect world up here, too. Honey bees are non-existent, bumble bees are small, and most of the pollination seems to be effected by a variety of boldly-striped hoverers and the beautifully iridescent flies that are ever associated with the blowing, munching and stamping cattle in the field beyond the hedge. I have clipped the hedge cautiously, aware there may still be active sparrows' nests, being careful to leave the pearl buds of the blackberries whose dark stains will follow those of the raspberries into the meringue nests so thoughtfully stocked by the village shop.

If I were to make the effort, nearby lanes and tracks offer bilberries (we called them whortleberries in our youth), hips, sloes and even the exquisite wild strawberries from which our domestic fruit sprang. And now is the time to collect the seeds of wild daisies, clover and burdock to adorn the garden next spring.

A little more effort might see me shunning work and stretching out among the heather and sheep-shorn grass of the mountain with just the liquid notes of the skylark and the lovely poems of Henry Kirke White to fill me with happy melancholia.

Footnote

They turned off the street lights in our cul-de-sac in November, having allowed them to banish the stars all through the summer nights. While I was gratified, I was also mystified. They have not come on again (it is February 2012 now). All the houses were built with one or more outside sensor-operated lights, so street lighting did not need to be installed in the first place. I fervently hope this trend will continue. My passion for the night sky is almost as strong as that for the countryside, having been given the Observer's Book of Astronomy as a child by my father, instantly turning Patrick Moore (now at last a Knight of the Realm) into one of my heroes.

Darkness is not to be feared; we only do so because the artificial sights, sounds and smells that have dulled our senses for generations cannot guide us. It is time we allowed those senses to recover – what an amazing world will be revealed.

THE JIG-SAW OF LIFE

18 July

A few minutes after clicking the Save button on my last entry I spotted the BBC's report on the street light dimming trial in Carmarthenshire. From 3,000 lights affected in the trial there were just 31 complaints. Perhaps, then, street lighting is not as popular as you'd think. But I have said enough on the matter. Good, you say.

Waiting for an opportunity to photograph the large flocks of garrulous rooks as they wheel and spin erratically across the sky is like waiting for Godot. There is an inexplicable menace in their passing, perhaps due to their sudden and random appearance and equally rapid disappearance, like a wolf spider across the carpet. I look up at them as my parents might have looked up at aerial combat in September 1940 when the harsh chatter of machine guns carried a far more dark foreboding.

The house-martins are quiet now that the insects are sheltering under the leaves, each drop of rain a bucketful to them. Even the ever-predatory magpies are silent, as are the comical sparrows and the watchful robin. As the misty rain slowly shrouds the distant slopes, the countryside around seems to settle into a waiting mode.

But much as I am preoccupied with observing our extraordinary wildlife, the ever-changing domestic plant and animal scene is also a constant source of delight. After a few days of welcome sunshine, the summer rain has intensified the colours in the garden. Throughout the spring and summer so far I have watched the hues change – from the whites and yellows of snowdrop, forsythia and loosestrife, the delicate blues of hosta and delphinium to the sweet pinks and reds of thyme, geranium, rose and fuchsia. Now the garden shouts with the Ferrari-scarlet of the *Crocosmia* and I express silent gratitude to the lady who planned and planted this garden and gave us this splendid and comforting outlook.

Beyond the mixed hedge with its dozen shades of green, cattle munch contentedly as they saunter among the growing thistles; somewhere a dog barks, glad of the postman's van to relieve his boredom; the percolator gurgles cheerfully; the oblivious traffic on the road through the village bustles about its business. The interlocking pieces of natural and man-made worlds could not fit together more perfectly.

Perhaps too perfectly, though, because last night our supposedly lovable, amenable and happy dog killed a hedgehog. He has barked at them before, so perhaps I should have recognised his behaviour this time. But he has never attacked them before. As soon as I realised he was actually at odds with something – I assumed a rat – I went to investigate, but I was too late: he had dispatched the poor animal, a nearly full-grown specimen, swiftly and efficiently as only a Jack Russell can. Full of remorse, I disposed of the body and sent the immensely pleased mutt indoors.

It was the first hedgehog I have seen since we moved here last year. They are not so common in this area as they are in Hampshire, where cars are their principal predators. And, apart from my sadness at this unnecessary death, it will be a great loss to the garden. The snuffling flea emporium, with its comical clockwork gait and insatiable appetite, is most welcome to share our small plot with us, but it seems that Sparky has other ideas. I shall have to be more watchful in future when he takes his midnight comfort break. He is already banned from the vegetable garden where there are sure to be voles and slowworms in the compost heap and under the broken pots.

It was a sad day, and I never did get that photograph of the raucous rooks. Somehow, a picture of a dead hedgehog does not seem appropriate for a diary that celebrates a love of the natural world. Some pieces of the jig-saw just never seem to fit.

Footnote

They say slowworms are rare; whether they are or not, it is quite right to protect them, but I don't believe they are rare. Nearly every garden has a small area where they can live and breed undisturbed, and they do, unnoticed. I used to have an old door lying in the garden, and sometimes I would gently lift it to see what was underneath. I was usually rewarded, examples being the vole above and slow worms below (the one with the dorsal stripe is female).

A HINT OF AUTUMN

6 August

Already the first hint of an approaching autumn was in the air as I watched the vague shape of a fox quartering the field beyond the hedge in the gathering gloom. I stood there quietly until the unhurried search among the tufts of grass was lost in the darkness. Sparky the hedgehog-slayer stood with me for a while but, seeing no point in it (a light breeze was blowing the fox's scent in the other direction), went back indoors to his warm blanket.

Autumn is a mixed blessing to me. We do not expect long, hot summers such as those we experienced when we lived on the Chichester Riviera all those years ago; at 700 feet up and so close to the western sea, spring can merge into fall with barely a respectable interval between. I will be sad to see the end of the startling *Crocosmia* 'Lucifer', the haute-couture feathers of the *Astilbe* and the sheer incongruity of the arum lilies.

But I will welcome the more natural sight of the browning of the bracken and the turning of the leaves even if the increasingly insistent west wind strips them all too soon and swirls them into the neat piles that form the winter home of the small furry creatures that live on the very edge of existence.

The sparrows and other birds feel the seasonal change, too. As the days shorten the search for food becomes slightly more urgent; the adolescent offspring still beg but their parents steadfastly ignore them; the martins fly ever lower, skimming the roofs for the cluster flies that seek shelter from the colder nights, and there is barely room for the family in the neat nest above the garage door. It will not be long before the sartorial migrants depart and I will supplement the diet of those who stay with the scraps from our table.

But autumn is not here yet; it is only the beginning of August. Summer may yet surprise us with the heat wave promised by the over-enthusiastic and over-paid television forecasters. I look up at the grey clouds punctuated by the occasional patch of blue and smile. I have not seen sixty-three summers without knowing that trying to forecast our maritime weather is futile. We must take each day as it comes and be thankful that we do not have to endure the extremes that give rise to so much tragedy in other corners of this restless world.

My life, too, is passing from summer to autumn; signs of senescence are in my hands, arms and face; digging is so much more tiring; the ability to plan is less easy, to think through problems more frustrating. Looking back is becoming more pleasing than looking forward and unfulfilled ambitions can now be shrugged away without regret. While it is hard not to rage against the price of the petrol, electricity and all the other things that we have become so utterly dependant upon, the beauty of the things around us, not least the ever-changing seasons, helps to soften our demeanour and lift our hearts.

Footnote

The picture is of one of my favourite trees; I photograph it nearly every time Sparky and I climb Frenni Fawr. With the Preseli Mountains dropping away to end dramatically at Dinas Head, down to the sunlit sea beyond, this solitary specimen epitomises all that is lovely about this part of Pembrokeshire

MAGICAL MOMENTS

1 September

I could easily believe in magic. Fluttering round the garden this morning was a female brimstone butterfly. It has been many years since I last saw one; my very well worn 1962 Observer's Book records it in a West Sussex village in May 1991. Brimstones, thought by some to be the origin of the word butterfly ('butter-coloured fly'), were very common when I was a child but, like most of our native butterflies, are now quite scarce. To me they have always been the very essence of those ephemeral creatures, not far removed from the fairies themselves, that brighten up our summer days and surprise us at other times.

As if that magical moment were not enough, I afterwards emptied out some rain water from the wheelbarrow and found a water beetle scuttling about in the bottom. They are common enough in streams and ponds (I always hope Sparky doesn't ingest any in his enthusiasm for drinking on our walks), but in wheelbarrows? I can only imagine that it mistook the water for a permanent fixture so I was sorry to disabuse it.

The setting sun last night was one of the best of the year; somewhere between fuchsia pink and blood red, it appeared briefly before setting at the very southern limit of the view from our garden. I whispered a quiet 'goodbye' and set my thoughts to other things until we see it again on its northern passage next year. If the setting sun is not magical, then I don't know what is.

Something else miraculous has happened, too; the runner beans I planted in the vegetable plot this year, wondering whether they would take in the cold wind that punctuate this altitude, have begun to produce pods. Not your bold, furry, voluptuous pods but long, thin apologies for what is probably my favourite vegetable (or is it a fruit?). They will be edible, nevertheless. Those I grew in the greenhouse have long since finished, their leaves turning brown in the inevitable slope towards the day when their stored goodness will be added to the compost bin, along with those tomato plants that have not succumbed to mosaic virus.

And the final small miracle – from underneath the lavender bush a small, pink rose has appeared, its sweet scent bringing back lovely memories, its delicate petals a reminder – if we needed it – of the magical fact that life, whatever form it takes, will find a way.

SUMMER'S END

25 September

Beyond the hedge the great ash tree's leaves are turning and in the garden it is now the seed heads that provide the most colour. The last of the butterflies, a small tortoiseshell, finds a single thrift flower to stave off death or hibernation for another day. House martins no longer call but hunt at rooftop height as they pack their bags for a long journey. The clouds are high but the air is heavy with moisture. Feverfew, foxglove and dandelion take over the vegetable patch and the pile of summer's garden debris is settling into what I hope will harbour hedgehogs, mice and slowworms over the coming winter. In the breeze, rose petals tiptoe across the gravel seeking a last resting place. Even if the calendar hadn't signalled the equinox during the past week, it is clear that autumn has arrived in earnest.

A black and ridiculously hairy caterpillar trudges slowly across the wall to a dark corner. Clacking magpies cheer the patio with blue iridescence and hooligan stare. No longer does the red kite drift leisurely above the fields in the mornings. The sheep seem to spend more time lying down now that their milk is no longer in constant demand, each in its own personal space, the flocks dotted across the fields just as a small child paints them with random splodges of white. Not for them the joined-at-the-hip jostling pigs or the cattle settling in a sunny corner looking for all the world as though they are enjoying a family picnic; each sheep munches quietly on its own with its own thoughts, ever-watchful for the wolves whose light tread has not graced this landscape for a thousand years.

Last night I dreamt I was trying to decide where to dig the pond. There was no reason why I should have such a dream: a pond? My head often says yes, but my back always says no. And yet the wish still lingers, if only to wake one morning to see a heron standing impassively, waiting for the first dim-witted snack to come within striking distance. On my walks in many counties of England and Wales I have marvelled at the patience and stillness of these birds; I too, am quiet and patient and so am eternally surprised and not a little disappointed that the only kingfisher I have seen is in the oriental print hanging on the bedroom wall. Fishermen see them often, no doubt, but I am a walker and not a sitter and consequently may live out my life without seeing the halcyon in the wild. That would be a shame.

Autumn is a time of goodbyes. Goodbye to the setting of the sun, although the astonishing evening displays continue. Photography cannot do justice to the violets, yellows, pinks and reds that in a painting would seem to leap from a fanciful artist's imagination. We have said a silent fond farewell to the swallows and swifts and bumble bees; even to some dear friends who have left a rich legacy of fond memories and distant laughter.

And yet while my eyes tell me that life seems to be ebbing from these ancient hills, my heart knows that this is but Nature's eventide; when her morning comes in March this beautiful countryside will stretch itself, as after a good night's sleep, and wake to another glorious day. It will be worth the wait. It always is.

Footnote

The sky can be magnificent at any time of the year; those magical clouds can present nature at its best, but sometimes modern technology can paint a wonderful picture, too. I often wonder where those planes are going...

THE PEACE OF THE NIGHT

1 October

The intermittent wind rustled the leaves of the eucalyptus tree as waves brush a shingle beach. It drew its invisible fingers across the top of the hedge as though flicking through the leaves of a favourite book, searching for a forgotten passage. Somewhere a sheep made a low guttural sound. The smell of grass and moor and sea wafted across my face in equal measure.

It was half past one in the morning. The sensible world was abed, but I stood in the garden in the mild night air and took in the scents and sounds and silences. Small rustlings at ground level told me that a wood mouse or hedgehog (if we have been blessed by a replacement) was quietly foraging, or a restless sparrow was seeking a warmer roost.

A lone yellow street light winked from the far hill. Above it, the palest grey light crept slowly from the north and came to rest over the fields. It may have been the aurora, hidden by the cloud cover, for the breeze was from the south west and the light was coming from the opposite direction. No star was visible. No moon rose to bathe the pasture with her ghostly light. The air was heavy and my mind emptied of all thought save one: that I was the only soul alive at that moment. I have had the feeling before, most recently when standing among the bluestones on Carn Menyn. It is a strange, out-of-body experience that is at once disturbing and yet comforting, and I held on to it for what seemed an age before I let it slip away again.

Such moments are rare; I was reluctant to return to the manufactured world behind me, so I stood there for longer than I had intended, letting the night draw out my inner warmth to bring me closer to equilibrium with the earth. But I did not feel cold; it was as if the darkness was a blanket, and the breeze filled with warming words. My senses became ever keener until I was sure I could hear the sound of breathing as the countryside slept.

As the stresses of the day melted away I caught myself smiling at nothing at all. And as Mother Nature drew her arms closer and closer around me, I was reminded that we all need to be embraced sometimes; and sometimes that just means going outside and allowing ourselves to be touched by the peace of the night.

Footnote

   Carn Menyn, the quarry from where those mysterious ancient people transported stones weighing several tons to Stonehenge, is accessible by bicycle, horse or foot and lies near the Golden Road, an ancient way that runs across the top of the Preseli Mountains. One of the things that particularly intrigues me is an old and rough-built enclosure that is colonised by lichens of many different and startling colours. I like to imagine that these slow-growing life-forms would have caused those ancient quarry-folk to stand and marvel just as I have. And perhaps they still do, even now.

IN A SENSE

22 October

Many of the natural sounds of the day are the same as those of the night – the robin still sings heartily, a lone gull calls from atop a street lamp and the paranoid wren still scolds an unseen foe; the bare hawthorn tree still mutters in a low voice as it scrapes against the fence and the breeze still rustles the few remaining leaves on the rowan. But hearing during the day is over-powered by sight, by far the most dominant of human senses, and the sounds of the countryside are pushed into the background.

The only way to remedy this is to close my eyes. Suddenly the signals to the other senses leap to the fore. It takes an effort to filter out the muffled sound of traffic, tractors and mowers, but eventually I find I can, for very short periods, focus in on the rest.

I hear a group of rooks passing from left to right, calling to each other. A buzz of wings in the opposite direction tells me the sparrows are moving to a different bush, or perhaps the blue tits are making their almost daily visit to enquire whether it isn't time to put out the feeders. An anonymous twittering starts up in next door's garden, probably signifying the ginger cat that hunts in these parts.

Closing my eyes encourages my mind to run off, like a wayward child, to poke its fingers into areas that may result in stings or other minor trauma, but it goes there anyway. It drifts into the past, with memories, good and bad, evoked by the senses that do not – cannot – stop taking in information. I try to empty my mind but it is supremely difficult; the click of the dog's claws on the paving intrude now – he is using his nose to look for places to reinforce his well-marked garden territory. He takes a deep, almost-silent breath and then noisily lets out the air through the flaps in the sides of his nostrils designed specifically so as not to disturb what he is sniffing.

Then the drip of water into the drain sets a metronomic rhythm that will soon find me unwittingly matching it to a favourite melody.

Now the breeze comes to my attention; the wind, of course, is in itself silent; it is only its passage past and through natural and man-made structures that gives it voice. It talks to the trees, fences and watering can in impartial harmony. And this rarely-ceasing movement of air that carries to me the smell of the soil, the heavy, sweet autumnal scent of decaying plants and the faintest hint of the salt water from the far side of the hills, shouts of autumn.

Eventually I have to open my eyes because I have lost all sense of balance, and I am rewarded with a magical rainbow. This sunshine-and-showers weather is perfect for sky-watching. As another black cloud rolls ponderously across the sky, one end of the rainbow can still be seen lancing into the hill to the north; then the whole is visible again, striking the ash tree with its jewelled wonder.

In the distance, seagulls' wings catch the light, too, twinkling like motes of dust in the early morning sun.

It all brings home to me the near-impossibility of separating out the senses, and how complex they are when working together, and how grateful I am to have all of them working in harmony. It reminds me that our senses are constantly gathering information, much of which hardly registers on our consciousness. No wonder dreams are so bizarre.

THE BIRDS

5 November

Starlings. Their coming in huge numbers heralds the coming of
something else – the coming of the end of the year. Down they came the
other day, in their hundreds. It is easy to over-estimate numbers of
moving creatures but when I looked at the photographs I had taken,
each showing only part of the flock, it was quite clear that there were
probably four to five hundred. They took over the field almost
completely. Every now and then perhaps fifty of them would take to the
air with a whirr like an infuriated gardener trying to start a recalcitrant
lawn mower.

Two pigeons often seen in the field watched and waited from a
nearby tree. A magpie about to fly across the field changed its mind and
turned back. Even the sheep seemed unsettled by this sudden
occupation as it stabbed at the ground with several hundred open beaks
as starlings do.

This morning two buzzards floated above our bungalows, attempting
to hover while they stared intently into the gardens. A herring gull, with
numerous empty fields to forage, took a particular dislike to a crow who
was minding its own business nearby, and pestered it until it flew away
to find food elsewhere. The gull, seemingly satisfied, flew off too, to
scream at nothing from a chimney pot.

The air is turning cold and this morning there was a hint of frost. Oil has been delivered. Winter clothes have replaced those of summer. The year is tumbling ever faster towards its fulfilment, and I have to feel a human sympathy for the cattle who, without the thick coats of the sheep, must rejoice each day that the sun shines on their backs.

But my sympathy is misplaced. Animals and birds have no compassion, only need. It is we humans, who by our works have assumed absolute power over this planet, that must show the compassion such power demands.

TO MARY

22 November

As autumn progresses inexorably towards winter the garden cries out for attention, and the birds cry out for food. The view across the hills, free of mist at last, twinkles through the jewelled lines of raindrops on the window. The hidden sun bathes the scene with hues that hint of coming snow, even as the tiny blue patches of sky wrestle for a place among the grey clouds.

Squadrons of starlings glide across my line of sight. A lone sparrow watches warily from the blackthorn. The sky begins to clear and the far fields take on a lighter green, promising a fine afternoon.

These days I am often woken around dawn by magpies noisily discussing their private business on the patio, but I don't mind. Better that than the harsh sounds of the past – the anonymous drone of commuter traffic, the echoing curses of dull oafs in the street or the strained and unsettling beat of someone else's radio. This is the country at its best and every natural sound reminds me why we settled here and sets my heart at peace.

The busy birds and mice have taken the last fruit from the gaunt blackberry briars, a signal that I must find something to help them through the cold nights to come. The easterly wind has completed the task of stripping the leaves from the trees who batten down their hatches for the long sleep. And even as we lose another friend, Mother Nature ceaselessly turns in her great cycle through the seasons. Could we imagine any other way?

Almost as if to reply, the words of Henry Kirke White come to me again:

Give me a cottage on some Cambrian wild,
Where, far from cities, I may spend my days,
And, by the beauties of the scene beguiled,
May pity man's pursuits, and shun his ways.
While on the rock I mark the browsing goat,
List to the mountain-torrent's distant noise,
Or the hoarse bittern's solitary note,
I shall not want the world's delusive joys;
But with my little scrip, my book, my lyre,
Shall think my lot complete, nor covet more;
And when, with time, shall wane the vital fire,
I'll raise my pillow on the desert shore,
And lay me down to rest, where the wild wave
Shall make sweet music o'er my lonely grave.

It is a rare poet who can contemplate the end of life without a hint of morbidity or self-pity. The beautiful simplicity of these lines elevates the writer – whose own life was so cruelly cut short in 1806 at the age of twenty-one – to the sublime state of immortality; would that we all could leave behind something as beautiful as this.

Perhaps we do, though: the happy memories that we create through our loves and friendships will outlast those of sadness, if we let them, and have the same eternal power as the promise of spring on such a bright autumnal day.

Footnote

I wasn't sure whether to publish this piece at all, in deference to the feelings of those who loved Mary and counted her as a friend. But death, as life, is something that touches us all; just as the new leaves will appear on the crab-apple tree each spring, perhaps each departed soul returns to the earth in some form to enrich it just as Mary has done. Some people believe this to be true; I can only hope it is.

LOOKING UP

One of the delights of autumn is the sheer number of birds that come to the feeder once we start putting out food in the colder weather. We stood at the window the other day and counted 42 sparrows, several chaffinches, blue tits, great tits, starlings and others. There must be a very efficient telegraph system among wild birds, because we normally only see a few regulars each day, searching the shrubs for something to eat. They love the wild bird seed but, surprisingly, show little enthusiasm for cornflakes.

Their aerial brilliance is staggering: hovering, even flying backwards, seems to take so little effort, and it is no wonder that man has always wanted to emulate them. We often talk of aircraft as birds, and their displays at air shows exhibit many of the characteristics of bird flight, albeit using unimaginable amounts of power to achieve what the birds do with the energy wrapped up in a few tiny seeds.

Could anything be more incongruous, though, than my passionate support of the continued flying of the majestic Avro Vulcan bomber and my more-than-passionate wonder of the nature unfolding in my modest garden? I am at least as thrilled by the aerial antics of the squabbling sparrows as I am by the 90 tons of ominous beauty that is the last of her kind to grace our skies. She is the rarest of birds.

Another rarity was in evidence the other evening when a pale and ghostly light hung over the darkening village. It was not just moonlight, for the moon was the thinnest silver crescent in the southern sky; it was the very last of the daylight reflecting from the disappearing cumulus cloud as it prepared to make way for the next bank of storm cloud rolling in from the west.

Rarely are we privileged to see such a dramatic and eerie sight as the day lingers beyond her allotted time and night waits in the wings for the conclusion of this final scene.

The reflected light from the moon at this time of the year is a splendid sight, especially if there are dark clouds for her to sail among – Alfred Noyes's *"The moon was a ghostly galleon, tossed upon cloudy seas"* could not have been better put in his poem *The Highwayman* which I learned by heart as a child. The drama of his work led me to the love of poetry that gave me hope, solace and laughter in the ensuing years.

We have had an extraordinary amount of rain in the past few weeks; it has raged down in sheets, thundering on the roof like the stampede of invisible herds; it has wafted as gently as the rustle of mice in the leaf litter that grows deeper by the day; but it has turned the hill fields a deeper shade of green.

I am sure wildlife does not like this weather, and nor do I; to me, however, it is merely a passing irritation – to them, a matter of survival. But, now we have reached the month that contains the shortest day, hope is already on the horizon. Things are already looking up.

Footnote

For more on Vulcan, see www.vulcantothesky.org/

WISHES

26 December

I wrote a long piece to mark the end of the year. Wittily entitled *Scents and sensibility*, it talked of my dislike of the smell of silage, my love of snow at the start of winter, and my hopes for the future – mine and those of others near and dear. It grew and grew. I was not happy with it; it happens sometimes. Foolishly thinking that the more I wrote, the more sensible and coherent it would become (whereas the opposite is usually true), I continued writing, and only made it worse.

So, I will salvage what I can, and leave the rest in my diary which contains all the fragments of poetry, prose and correspondence that someone else will have to decide to keep or discard, as they judge best. Sadly, the sheer volume of my unpublished writing makes me doubt that anyone will have the time, even if they had the inclination.

Our robin (as we like to refer to him) continues to sing in the dead of night as well as during the day, and I do wonder when he sleeps. While birds do not enjoy a good night's sleep as we would know it, they must rest, and I am unable to understand how this particular bird, loved of the Christmas card designer, gets any rest at all. All I know is, his song echoing in the stillness at one o'clock in the morning helps me to drop off without any trouble at all.

The selfish hope for snow receded as the first few days of winter brought more rain, higher temperatures and a warm, wet wind – such a contrast to this time last year. Yet there was, for a few days this month, that slight yellowness in the sky that foretells the coming of snow. It was as beautiful as it was ominous; ominous, that is, if you do not feel comfortable on the white stuff. Still being, most of the time, relatively steady on my feet, I look forward to its gentle falling with the child-like excitement that I have never lost in all the years of my life. There is in my view no better way to round off the year. But this year that wish has not been fulfilled.

So to other wishes. With the days now beginning imperceptibly to lengthen, the first full set of seasons in our cosy bungalow is complete. The first year in a new home is always full of surprises, and anticipating their return in the seasons to come an added pleasure. I look forward to the return of the jewels in the snow, the fox on the mountain and the special sunsets with equal eagerness. Even the inevitable disappointments and sad times that measure our lives are part of the same tapestry; I treat with reverence every moment that passes, and hope I will do so until the last of them slides into view. If in that last moment I can again see a circle of sunlight fall upon the merlins' hill, or hear robin redbreast pour out his song in the still of the starry night - and if I can also know that I have been able to tell you about it - then it will have been a life worth living.

Until then, though, my most ardent wishes are for those human friends who are looking to the new year with a measure of anxiety or concern. May we all treasure each year's end, not as a conclusion, but as the beginning of a new chapter full of positive thoughts for better health, deeper happiness and simple adventures.

Footnote: The jewels in the snow

In December 2010 I wrote to a friend: "When we turned out the lights last night we were treated to the most magical show of the moonlight creating a myriad tiny jewels in the snow. We could only marvel, and I could only wonder at those who spend a fortune trying to create the effect that they could have seen without using electricity. The wonder of nature will always trump the ingenuity of man."

I wish everyone who reads this book peace and joy as plentiful as the gems in the moonlit snow. Writing it has been an enormous pleasure and I can hardly wait until I have another year's worth of views from the hills to put together.

And here they are:

Volume 2 (2012 Views)
and
Volume 3 (2013 Views)

Available from Amazon now

See also the beginning of this book for my other publications

Afterword

MUSIC OF THE SPHERE

The plink of rain into a silver pool;
The song of the thrush, clearly in the cool
Air after the storm; the chirping cricket;
The mild bee, droning in the gorse thicket.

When the day dies, and the splendid sun yields
And night, like rain, makes black pools in the fields
The owl, from a dead elm, hoots once, twice – stops,
Awaits the ghostly answer from the copse.

Far, beneath gaunt cliffs, waves are restless, too,
Embroidering with white the endless blue,
Murmuring, whispering, until the dawn
Breaks to the lark, our unfailing alarm.

Hear the music of this silver sphere – Earth –
More than a hundred thousand Steinways' worth.

This sonnet, and 51 others, are available as an e book from Amazon

www.ingramcontent.com/pod-product-compliance
Lightning Source LLC
Chambersburg PA
CBHW050820290526
45792CB00001B/191